S0-DJF-267

My Year in Baseball

A Sports Record Book

WARNER TREASURES™
Published by Warner Books
A Time Warner Company

Warner Treasures is a trademark of Warner Books, Inc.

Warner Books, Inc.,
1271 Avenue of the Americas
New York, NY 10020

 A Time Warner Company

Book design by Leandra Jones
Cover design by Lisa C. McGarry
Baseball illustration by Sharon T. Moccia

My Year in Baseball is produced by becker&mayer!, Ltd.

Printed in Singapore.
First Printing: March 1996
10 9 8 7 6 5 4 3 2 1

ISBN: 0-446-91132-1

My Year in Baseball

in

Baseball

A Sports Record Book

by _____

My Year in Baseball

What better way to keep track of your progress through the upcoming season than by keeping a diary of your team's successes!

All you have to do is carefully observe every game you play in—and then, after the game is over, take a few moments to fill in the blanks on the pages for that game. Do this after every game and, by the time the season wraps up, you'll have a permanent diary of your year in baseball.

It's easy, fun to do, and best of all, by writing a complete record of your sports season you're writing your own book! When the season comes to an end, you'll be able to place your diary in a treasured spot on your bookshelf.

Be sure to write your name on the title page of your sports journal. After all, how many kids your age can claim to have written a book?

MY YEAR IN BASEBALL

Year: _____

My name: _____

My team's name: _____

My coach's name: _____

My uniform number: _____

My team's league: _____

My height: _____

My weight: _____

MY TEAMMATES

_____

_____

_____

_____

_____

_____

_____

_____

_____

_____

Date _____

1 GAME

Final score _____

Our Opponent: _____

Positions I played: _____
_____

Plays I made well: _____
_____

Things I need to work on: _____
_____
_____

The best part of today's game: _____
_____
_____

**What the coach told me about
my performance:** _____
_____

Catching Flies

Too often, when running after a fly ball, outfielders will put their head down and lose sight of the ball. To correct this problem, always try to run on the balls of your feet. It will keep your head steady and your eyes focused on the flight of the ball, making it much easier to track down and catch.

"Say a prayer before you start each game. Don't pray that you'll win the game. Just pray that when you get out there on the field, you'll be the best you can be."

ROY CAMPANELLA
Hall of Fame catcher

Game 1

MY SEASON SO FAR

As a hitter: ## As a pitcher:

At bats _____   Innings pitched _____

Hits _____   Wins _____

Batting avg. _____   Losses _____

Bases on balls _____   Saves _____

Doubles _____   Earned runs _____

Triples _____   Earned run avg. _____

Home runs _____   Strikeouts _____

Runs scored _____   Bases on balls _____

Runs batted in _____   Stolen bases _____

Team record _____

Perfect Your Pitching Motion

One of the best ways to improve your pitching motion is by practicing in front of a full-length mirror. Get in the habit of watching yourself from a full windup, as well as from a stretch position. Even better, turn sideways and practice your pick-off move to first base.

By practicing these motions, you'll get a much better idea of what the batter and runner see when you're on the mound.

"To be good in baseball, you've gotta have a lot of little boy in you."

ROY CAMPANELLA

_____
Date

2
GAME

_____
Final score

Our Opponent: _____

Positions I played: _____

_____

Plays I made well: _____

_____

Things I need to work on: _____

_____

_____

The best part of today's game: _____

_____

_____

What the coach told me about
my performance: _____

_____

Sunglasses on the Field

Sunglasses have become a standard part of a defensive player's equipment. Most players wear wraparound shades. If you decide to wear sunglasses when in the field, be certain that they fit snugly enough so that they don't fall off when you're running after a fly ball or pop-up.

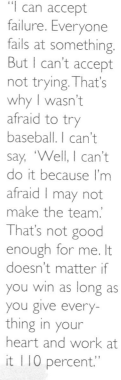

"I can accept failure. Everyone fails at something. But I can't accept not trying. That's why I wasn't afraid to try baseball. I can't say, 'Well, I can't do it because I'm afraid I may not make the team.' That's not good enough for me. It doesn't matter if you win as long as you give everything in your heart and work at it 110 percent."

MICHAEL JORDAN

NBA player and former minor league outfielder

Game 2

MY SEASON SO FAR

As a hitter:
● ● ● ● ● ● ● ● ● ● ● ● ● ●

At bats _____

Hits _____

Batting avg. _____

Bases on balls _____

Doubles _____

Triples _____

Home runs _____

Runs scored _____

Runs batted in _____

As a pitcher:
● ● ● ● ● ● ● ● ● ● ● ●

Innings pitched _____

Wins _____

Losses _____

Saves _____

Earned runs _____

Earned run avg. _____

Strikeouts _____

Bases on balls _____

Stolen bases _____

Team record _____

Strengthen Your Wrists!

One of the best ways to improve your game is by strengthening your wrists, and to do that all you really need is an ordinary tennis ball. Squeeze the tennis ball ten times in a row with one hand, and then do the same thing with the ball in your other hand. Do this as often as you can. You'll soon feel the difference in your wrists when you swing a bat or throw a pitch.

"A critic once characterized baseball as six minutes of action crammed into two-and-one-half hours."

RAY FITZGERALD
Boston Globe
columnist

3

GAME

Our Opponent: _____

Positions I played: _____

_____

Plays I made well: _____

_____

Things I need to work on: _____

_____

_____

The best part of today's game: _____

_____

_____

**What the coach told me about
my performance:** _____

_____

How to Throw a Four-Seamer

If you want to make your pitches go straight and not tail off, throw a four-seamer—grip the ball across four of the red seams. (If you can't grip all four seams, two seams will also do).

On the other hand, if you do want to make the ball tail away, grip it without your fingers touching any of the seams. Your throw will have the same speed, but the ball will dip and dive just as it reaches the plate.

"The umpires always say 'Play ball.' They don't say 'Work ball.'"

WILLIE STARGELL
former Pittsburgh Pirates slugger

MY SEASON SO FAR

As a hitter:

At bats _____

Hits _____

Batting avg. _____

Bases on balls _____

Doubles _____

Triples _____

Home runs _____

Runs scored _____

Runs batted in _____

As a pitcher:

Innings pitched _____

Wins _____

Losses _____

Saves _____

Earned runs _____

Earned run avg. _____

Strikeouts _____

Bases on balls _____

Stolen bases _____

Team record _____

Buy a Glove That's the Right Size

Be careful not to purchase a fielder's glove that's too big for you. You want a glove that's just your size and flexible to use. A glove that's too big will be hard to handle in the field.

"Baseball is ninety percent mental. The other half is physical."

ANONYMOUS

Date _____

GAME 4

Final score _____

Our Opponent: _____

Positions I played: _____

_____

Plays I made well: _____

_____

Things I need to work on: _____

_____

_____

The best part of today's game: _____

_____

_____

**What the coach told me about
my performance:** _____

_____

What to Chew These Days

Ballplayers like to chew when they're playing. But in recent years, minor league ballplayers have been ordered not to chew tobacco because it can lead to cancer. If you want to chew something during a game, get the hang of eating sunflower seeds. They're a popular, healthy replacement for tobacco.

Try one seed at first. It takes some time to learn how to crack open the seed with your teeth. But once you get the hang of it, you'll find that it's great fun—and healthy, too.

"You gotta have a catcher. If you don't have a catcher, you'll have all passed balls."

CASEY STENGEL

Hall of Fame manager

Game

MY SEASON SO FAR

As a hitter: **As a pitcher:**

● ●

At bats _____   Innings pitched _____

Hits _____   Wins _____

Batting avg. _____   Losses _____

Bases on balls _____   Saves _____

Doubles _____   Earned runs _____

Triples _____   Earned run avg. _____

Home runs _____   Strikeouts _____

Runs scored _____   Bases on balls _____

Runs batted in _____   Stolen bases _____

Team record _____

Get a Proper Grip on Your Bat

When gripping a bat, be certain to get in the habit of holding the bat in your fingers—not in the palm of your hand.

Most new players hold the bat in their palms, which not only cuts down on their bat speed, but also can be quite painful if they get jammed by a pitch.

"A full mind is an empty bat."

BRANCH RICKEY

former St. Louis Cardinals manager and Hall of Famer

_____
Date

5
GAME

_____
Final score

Our Opponent: _____

Positions I played: _____
_____

Plays I made well: _____
_____

Things I need to work on: _____
_____

_____

The best part of today's game: _____
_____

_____

What the coach told me about
my performance: _____

_____

Don't be Bashful

Get in the habit of yelling, "I got it!" when running for a pop-up or fly ball. Many people are too timid to do this at first, but it's absolutely essential if you don't want any of your teammates crashing in to you.

Remember: the louder you are, the better.

"How can you think and hit at the same time?"

YOGI BERRA
Hall of Fame catcher

Game 5

MY SEASON SO FAR

As a hitter:

At bats _____

Hits _____

Batting avg. _____

Bases on balls _____

Doubles _____

Triples _____

Home runs _____

Runs scored _____

Runs batted in _____

As a pitcher:

Innings pitched _____

Wins _____

Losses _____

Saves _____

Earned runs _____

Earned run avg. _____

Strikeouts _____

Bases on balls _____

Stolen bases _____

Team record _____

Keep Count of the Outs

After each out is recorded make certain to remind your teammates of how many outs there are. Games are lost too many times because some fielder forgot how many outs there were.

Don't let this happen to you!

"A complete ballplayer today is one who can hit, field, run, throw, and pick the right agent."

BOB LURIE
San Francisco Giants owner

Date _____

GAME 6

Final score _____

Our Opponent: _____

Positions I played: _____

_____

Plays I made well: _____

_____

Things I need to work on: _____

_____

_____

The best part of today's game: _____

_____

_____

**What the coach told me about
my performance:** _____

_____

Sliding Tips

When sliding, many players scrape their hands or knees. To prevent this, get in the habit of holding a batting glove in each hand when you run the bases. Then, when you slide, there won't be any temptation to open your hands up and scrape your palms as you slide.

To protect your knee from being bruised, consider wearing a basketball kneepad under your pant's leg on the knee where you slide the most. If a kneepad is too big or bulky, wrap your knee with an elastic bandage before every game. That will protect your knee from bumps and bruises, but— more importantly—won't cut down on your speed.

"If horses don't eat it, I don't want to play on it."

RICHIE "DICK" ALLEN

former White Sox first baseman, talking about artificial turf

Game 6

MY SEASON SO FAR

As a hitter:

●●●●●●●●●●●

At bats _____

Hits _____

Batting avg. _____

Bases on balls _____

Doubles _____

Triples _____

Home runs _____

Runs scored _____

Runs batted in _____

As a pitcher:

●●●●●●●●●●●

Innings pitched _____

Wins _____

Losses _____

Saves _____

Earned runs _____

Earned run avg. _____

Strikeouts _____

Bases on balls _____

Stolen bases _____

Team record _____

Taking a Lead Off Base

When taking a lead, make sure your knees are bent, your body is stable, and you can either move quickly back to the base you're on, or toward the next base.

Above all, keep your hands off your knees! If your hands are on your knees, then you're basically telling the pitcher that you're not threatening to run. Keep your hands to the sides, ready to help you move in either direction.

"The game isn't over till it's over."

YOGI BERRA

_____

Date

7

GAME

Final score

Our Opponent: _____

Positions I played: _____

_____

Plays I made well: _____

_____

Things I need to work on: _____

_____

_____

The best part of today's game: _____

_____

_____

**What the coach told me about
my performance:** _____

_____

On Anger...

All baseball players know what it's like to be frustrated. Too many players throw their batting helmets —or even their bats—in disgust.

Don't be one of those players. Show self-control. Develop a sense of self-discipline. Understand that the game will be frustrating at times. But there's no reason to throw anything just because you're angry. Even worse, an umpire can toss you out of the game for doing such things.

Ask yourself: Why is it so hard to control my emotions? And if I can't, who will?

"The trick is growing up without growing old."

CASEY STENGEL

Game 7

MY SEASON SO FAR

As a hitter:

At bats _____

Hits _____

Batting avg. _____

Bases on balls _____

Doubles _____

Triples _____

Home runs _____

Runs scored _____

Runs batted in _____

As a pitcher:

Innings pitched _____

Wins _____

Losses _____

Saves _____

Earned runs _____

Earned run avg. _____

Strikeouts _____

Bases on balls _____

Stolen bases _____

Team record _____

Bumblebees in Your Bat

Any ballplayer who has ever played ball in cold weather can describe the sting of swinging an icy bat with cold hands at a hot pitch. Some players refer to the painful sensation as having "bees in one's bat."

There really is no cure for this problem, but there are some things you can do to help prevent the situation. First, be certain to wear batting gloves on both hands when hitting. Second, on cold and raw days, bring along a hot water thermos to keep your hands warm on the bench.

Remember: The warmer your hands are when you hit, the less chance of "bees in your bat."

"You spend a good piece of your life gripping a baseball and in the end it turns out that it was the other way around all the time."

JIM BOUTON

former New York Yankees pitcher, author of Ball Four

_____ _____

Date **8 GAME** **Final score**

Our Opponent: _____

Positions I played: _____

_____

Plays I made well: _____

_____

Things I need to work on: _____

_____

_____

The best part of today's game: _____

_____

_____

**What the coach told me about
my performance:** _____

_____

Putting Down a Bunt

Many experts say bunting is a lost art. That's too bad, because if you can bunt, you can manu- facture at least one hit a game for yourself.

To bunt for a hit, all you need is a good batting eye, the ability to get your bat out in front of the plate, and an ability to push the bunt either down the third base- line or up the first baseline.

What most players don't realize is that you don't have to be the fastest player in the world to be a good bunter. It's the element of surprise that's most important.

And, you don't have to bunt the very first pitch in the count. Wait until the count is two balls and no strikes. That's a better time to surprise your opponents.

"I went through life as the 'player to be named later.' "

JOE GARAGIOLA

former catcher and sportscaster

Game 8

MY SEASON SO FAR

As a hitter: As a pitcher:

● ●

At bats _____   Innings pitched _ _ _

Hits _____   Wins _____

Batting avg. _____   Losses _ _ _____

Bases on balls _____   Saves _____

Doubles _____   Earned runs _____

Triples _____   Earned run avg. _____

Home runs _____   Strikeouts _____

Runs scored _____   Bases on balls _____

Runs batted in _____   Stolen bases _____

Team record _____

Strengthening Your Arm

The best—and safest—way to make your throwing arm stronger is to go to the outfield with a teammate and practice throwing to each other over a long distance.

Start close together, no more than 20 feet apart. Then as you gradually warm up, begin to back up. Keep throwing to each other on the fly so that you begin to use more and more arm strength.

As you continue to move apart, you'll find that you have to throw with your arm in a direct, over-hand motion. That's how you'll strengthen your arm muscles.

Follow this routine for twenty minutes every day, and before you know it, you'll be surprised at how much stronger your arm has become.

"When I started, baseball was played by nine tough competitors on grass in beautiful ballparks. By the time I was finished, there were 10 men on each side, the game was played indoors, on plastic, and I had to spend half of my time watching out for a man dressed in a chicken suit who kept trying to kiss me."

RON LUCIANO
former major league umpire

_____   **GAME 9**   _____

Date   **Final score**

Our Opponent: _____

Positions I played: _____

_____

Plays I made well: _____

_____

Things I need to work on: _____

_____

_____

The best part of today's game: _____

_____

_____

**What the coach told me about
my performance:** _____

_____

Stealing a Base

If your league allows you to steal bases, by all means learn and practice this important offensive skill. You should never take a lead so far off the base that you can't get back before the pitcher's pick-off throw arrives. And unless you're planning on stealing a base on that very pitch, you should always shift your weight evenly so that you can move quickly in either direction.

When you do decide to steal, do not hesitate! Run all out to the next base! Whoever hesitates will be out. And always make certain to slide! Don't go to a base standing up—you never know when that throw from the catcher might arrive there first!

"Us ballplayers do things backward. First we play, then we retire and go to work."

CHARLIE GEHRINGER

Hall of Fame second baseman

Game 9

MY SEASON SO FAR

As a hitter: ## As a pitcher:

● ● ● ● ● ● ● ● ● ● ● ● ● ● ● ● ● ● ● ●

At bats _____   Innings pitched _____

Hits _____   Wins _____

Batting avg. _____   Losses _____

Bases on balls _____   Saves _____

Doubles _____   Earned runs _____

Triples _____   Earned run avg. _____

Home runs _____   Strikeouts _____

Runs scored _____   Bases on balls _____

Runs batted in _____   Stolen bases _____

Team record _____

Making the Pivot

The double-play pivot at second base involves skill, coordination, and courage. Above all, you should stay out of the way of the advancing base runner. Second, try to receive the ball with both hands.

Keep your weight balanced on both knees so that you can anticipate a bad throw (it's easier to adjust to a good throw than to a bad one).

Practice getting the ball out of your glove as quickly as you can. It helps to have a glove with a broken-in pocket so that you can feel the ball when you catch it.

Once you have made your pivot, get out of the play quickly. Most second base collisions occur after the pivot has been made.

"A waist is a terrible thing to mind."

TERRY FORSTER

overweight former pitcher, Atlanta Braves

Date _____

GAME 10

Final score _____

Our Opponent: _____

Positions I played: _____

_____

Plays I made well: _____

_____

Things I need to work on: _____

_____

_____

The best part of today's game: _____

_____

_____

**What the coach told me about
my performance:** _____

_____

Arguing with Umpires

Going jaw-to-jaw with an umpire may seem like a time-honored tradition in baseball, but as any major leaguer will tell you, the simple fact of the matter is that umpires usually make the right call. And to that end, umps deserve to be treated with respect.

Rather than looking upon the umpire as a necessary evil, try striking up a friendly conversation with him or her during the course of a game. Not only will you find most umps to be pleasant people, but you'll also find yourself thinking twice before wanting to get into an argument.

Most important to remember: umpires never lose arguments!

"Tony Gwynn was named Player of the Year for the month of April."

RALPH KINER
Hall of Famer and New York Mets sportscaster

Game

MY SEASON SO FAR

As a hitter: As a pitcher:
●●●●●●●●●●●●●●●●●●●●●●

At bats _____   Innings pitched _____

Hits _____   Wins _____

Batting avg. _____   Losses _____

Bases on balls _____   Saves _____

Doubles _____   Earned runs _____

Triples _____   Earned run avg. _____

Home runs _____   Strikeouts _____

Runs scored _____   Bases on balls _____

Runs batted in _____   Stolen bases _____

Team record _____

Learn to Switch-Hit

One of the best skills you can learn early on is how to switch-hit. Don't wait until you're set in your habits. Start now, when you can develop your ability to hit from both sides of the plate.

All it takes is some discipline and a desire to get better. Practice your swing from both sides of the plate, and practice as often as you can. Understand that your "other" side is going to feel weak, goofy, and strange at the start. But with each practice swing, you'll become that much stronger and more comfortable with your new approach to hitting.

"I remember one time going out to the mound to talk with (Hall of Fame pitcher) Bob Gibson. He told me to get back behind the plate, that the only thing I knew about pitching was that it was hard to hit."

TIM MCCARVER

former catcher for the St. Louis Cardinals and sportscaster

_____   _____
Date   **GAME 11**   **Final score**

Our Opponent: _____

Positions I played: _____

_____

Plays I made well: _____

_____

Things I need to work on: _____

_____

_____

The best part of today's game: _____

_____

_____

**What the coach told me about
my performance:** _____

_____

The Legacy of Jackie Robinson

There was a time when African-American ballplayers weren't allowed to play in the major leagues. Undaunted by this ruling, the best African-American players played in the Negro Leagues. These leagues were in existence from the 1920s to the 1950s.

In 1947, Jackie Robinson, who was a standout football, basketball, and baseball player at UCLA, was asked to play in the major leagues with the Brooklyn Dodgers. Robinson was a terrific ballplayer—he made the Hall of Fame—but even more than his contribution on the field, Robinson is still today recognized for his courage, grace, and steady demeanor as an athlete and gentleman.

"Baseball is the only field of endeavor where a man can succeed three times out of ten and be considered a good performer."

TED WILLIAMS
Hall of Famer

Game 11

MY SEASON SO FAR

As a hitter:	**As a pitcher:**
At bats _____	Innings pitched _____
Hits _____	Wins _____
Batting avg. _____	Losses _____
Bases on balls _____	Saves _____
Doubles _____	Earned runs _____
Triples _____	Earned run avg. _____
Home runs _____	Strikeouts _____
Runs scored _____	Bases on balls _____
Runs batted in _____	Stolen bases _____

Team record _____

The Story Behind Pine Tar

Ever notice how major leaguers always put black, sticky stuff on their bat? That stuff is pine tar, and as you might imagine, it comes directly from the sap of pine trees and is extremely sticky!

Ballplayers pour some of the pine tar onto a rag, and then carefully dab a bit of it onto their bats. They use it to keep their grip on the bats, especially when it's hot and their hands are sweaty and slippery.

You can use pine tar on *your* bat as well. Just remember that it's unbelievably sticky and that it's very hard to remove from your clothing and hands.

"Baseball is a game where a curve is an optical illusion, a screwball can be a pitch or a person, stealing is legal, and you can spit anywhere you like except in the umpire's eye or on the ball."

JIM MURRAY
Pulitzer Prize–winning sports columnist

_____
Date

GAME

_____
Final score

Our Opponent: _____

Positions I played: _____

_____

Plays I made well: _____

_____

Things I need to work on: _____

_____

_____

The best part of today's game: _____

_____

_____

**What the coach told me about
my performance:** _____

_____

Metal vs. Rubber Spikes

In most youth baseball leagues metal spikes are not only discouraged, they're usually illegal! In an effort to avoid injuries, metal spikes are generally outlawed.

There's no reason you can't play just as well with baseball shoes that feature rubberized spikes. You can still dig in at the plate, toe the rubber on the mound properly, and get plenty of speed on the base paths.

You may like the sound that metal spikes make when walking on pavement or the sidewalk, but in the long run you're a lot safer with the rubberized spikes.

"The only way to prove you're a good sport is to lose."

ERNIE BANKS
Hall of Famer

Game 12

MY SEASON SO FAR

As a hitter:

As a pitcher:

● ●

At bats _____   Innings pitched _____

Hits _____   Wins _____

Batting avg. _____   Losses _____

Bases on balls _____   Saves _____

Doubles _____   Earned runs _____

Triples _____   Earned run avg. _____

Home runs _____   Strikeouts _____

Runs scored _____   Bases on balls _____

Runs batted in _____   Stolen bases _____

Team record _____

Getting Ready in the On-Deck Circle

This is the time when you should really begin to focus on the pitcher and what kind of windup he has and what kind of pitch he throws. If you're not paying attention to what's going on, then there's a good chance that the pitcher may fool you when you come to your turn at the plate.

Loosen up in the on-deck circle by swinging a weighted bat. (Be careful to make certain none of your teammates are standing behind you!) While swinging the weighted bat, pretend you're at the plate, facing the pitcher. When it's your turn to hit, take your game bat with you and stride to the batter's box with confidence.

"Baseball is like church. Many attend, but few understand."

WES WESTRUM
former major league manager

Date

GAME 13

Final score

Our Opponent: _____

Positions I played: _____

_____

Plays I made well: _____

_____

Things I need to work on: _____

_____

_____

The best part of today's game: _____

_____

_____

What the coach told me about my performance: _____

_____

A Walk is as Good as a Hit!

For some reason many young ballplayers don't like to get walks. To them, it's an insult that the pitcher didn't throw a pitch they could hit.

It's okay to have so much confidence in your ability to hit that you feel a little frustrated by getting a walk, but remember that the purpose of the game is to get on base—it doesn't really make any difference whether you get to first base from a hit, walk, or an error.

Once on base, you're in a position to help your ballclub win the game by scoring a run. That's why smart baseball people—and unselfish teammates—recognize that a walk is just as good as a hit.

"If Casey Stengel were alive today, he'd be spinning in his grave."

RALPH KINER

Game 13

MY SEASON SO FAR

As a hitter:

● ● ● ● ● ● ● ● ● ● ● ● ●

At bats _____

Hits _____

Batting avg. _____

Bases on balls _____

Doubles _____

Triples _____

Home runs _____

Runs scored _____

Runs batted in _____

As a pitcher:

● ● ● ● ● ● ● ● ● ● ● ● ●

Innings pitched _____

Wins _____

Losses _____

Saves _____

Earned runs _____

Earned run avg. _____

Strikeouts _____

Bases on balls _____

Stolen bases _____

Team record _____

Throwing Strikes

It doesn't make any difference how fast you can throw a ball if you can't throw the ball over the plate for strikes.

The pitcher's purpose is just that: to throw strikes. Otherwise, your opponents will simply wait you out to draw a base on balls. Even worse, your teammates in the field will begin to grumble.

To practice, find a brick wall somewhere near your home, walk off the distance between home-plate and the pitcher's rubber, and go to work. Pretend you're pitching to real players and work each batter with a ball-and-strike count. Make every pitch count. Learn to make adjustments in order to throw the ball in the strike zone.

"Most batting slumps are like the common cold. They last two weeks, no matter what you do."

TERRY KENNEDY
former major league catcher

Date _____

GAME 14

Final score _____

Our Opponent: _____

Positions I played: _____
_____

Plays I made well: _____
_____

Things I need to work on: _____
_____
_____

The best part of today's game: _____
_____
_____

**What the coach told me about
my performance:** _____
_____

Skills for Catchers

First, never turn your head when a pitch comes in or bounces in the dirt. All of your equipment is designed to protect you, but only if you face forward. Keep your nongloved hand behind your back when the pitch comes in—there's less of a chance that a foul tip might hit it.

On pop-ups, take your mask off and only toss it away from you once you have found where the ball is. Look out for teammates who are also chasing that pop fly.

Make sure your throwing arm is warmed up. Be sure to make a throw to second base before the start of each inning, just to keep your arm loose and ready to go.

"Statistics are used by baseball fans in much the same way that a drunk leans against a street lamp; it's there more for support than for enlightenment."

VIN SCULLY

Los Angeles Dodgers broadcaster

14

Game

MY SEASON SO FAR

As a hitter:

● ● ● ● ● ● ● ● ● ● ● ● ● ●

At bats _____

Hits _____

Batting avg. _____

Bases on balls _____

Doubles _____

Triples _____

Home runs _____

Runs scored _____

Runs batted in _____

As a pitcher:

● ● ● ● ● ● ● ● ● ● ●

Innings pitched _____

Wins _____

Losses _____

Saves _____

Earned runs _____

Earned run avg. _____

Strikeouts _____

Bases on balls _____

Stolen bases _____

Team record _____

Using a Batting Tee

One of the very best ways to improve your stroke is by using a batting tee. It's so popular that many major leaguers still use a batting tee every day, right before batting practice.

A batting tee allows you to refine your swing. Since the ball is not moving, you can truly concentrate on every part of your stance: where your feet are, the position of your hands, your weight balance, everything. Then, by simply concentrating on the ball, you can get into the habit of making contact just the way you want to.

The theory is quite simple yet solid: the more you swing properly during practice, the more likely you are to swing properly during a game.

"It was so hot today, the fire hydrants were chasing the dogs."

DOUG FLYNN
former major league infielder

_____ **Date**

_____ **Final score**

Our Opponent: _____

Positions I played: _____

_____

Plays I made well: _____

_____

Things I need to work on: _____

_____

_____

The best part of today's game: _____

_____

_____

**What the coach told me about
my performance:** _____

_____

The Truth Behind Superstitions

Every ballplayer seems to have some sort of superstition or type of behavior that he or she repeats every day on the ballfield to "insure" that he or she will have good luck.

Example: when some players are in a hot streak at the plate, they'll keep wearing the same undershirt, day after day. Or they'll take just three practice swings—no more and no less.

Pitchers won't step on the foul line. Or they'll wear their cap a certain way.

Do superstitions work? Well, maybe. Are they harmful? No, probably not. Only you can determine whether they work for you.

"Every season has its peaks and valleys. What you have to try to eliminate is the Grand Canyon."

ANDY VAN SLYKE
major league outfielder

15
Game

MY SEASON SO FAR

As a hitter: ## As a pitcher:

● ●

At bats _____   Innings pitched _____

Hits _____   Wins _____

Batting avg. _____   Losses _____

Bases on balls _____   Saves _____

Doubles _____   Earned runs _____

Triples _____   Earned run avg. _____

Home runs _____   Strikeouts _____

Runs scored _____   Bases on balls _____

Runs batted in _____   Stolen bases _____

Team record _____

Picking Up Grounders

The best practice for infielders is to pick up as many grounders as you can.

Stand about 20 feet away from a brick wall and throw a tennis ball at the wall. Throw the ball so that when it bounces back to you, it's low to the ground like a real ground ball.

Start to field. Don't even use your fielder's glove. Pick the ball up with your bare hands and throw it back against the wall. Repeat over and over. Within 15 minutes you'll field close to 100 ground balls. And if you can catch a bouncing tennis ball with your bare hands, just imagine how easy it will be to catch a real grounder in a game with your glove on!

"On paper, our team looks real good. It's just too bad we play our games on grass and not cardboard."

ANONYMOUS BASEBALL MANAGER

Date

Final score

Our Opponent: _____

Positions I played: _____
_____

Plays I made well: _____
_____

Things I need to work on: _____
_____
_____

The best part of today's game: _____
_____
_____

**What the coach told me about
my performance:** _____
_____

Batting Helmets

In all youth baseball leagues, the rules stipulate that every batter has to wear a batting helmet. Most helmets come with earflaps on both sides of the helmet.

The helmet you wear should fit snugly, but it should not be too tight! It should also not be so loose that when you run it bounces on your head or falls off.

When you're on the base paths, remember that it can be difficult to hear your coaches when wearing a helmet, especially when you're on second base. Since you can't take the helmet off, pick up on what your coach is saying by trying to face him as best you can.

"I could never play in New York. The first time I ever came into a game there, I got into the bullpen car and they told me to lock the doors."

MIKE FLANAGAN
former major league pitcher

16
Game

MY SEASON SO FAR

As a hitter:

● ● ● ● ● ● ● ● ● ● ● ● ●

At bats _____

Hits _____

Batting avg. _____

Bases on balls _____

Doubles _____

Triples _____

Home runs _____

Runs scored _____

Runs batted in _____

As a pitcher:

● ● ● ● ● ● ● ● ● ● ● ● ●

Innings pitched _____

Wins _____

Losses _____

Saves _____

Earned runs _____

Earned run avg. _____

Strikeouts _____

Bases on balls _____

Stolen bases _____

Team record _____

When is a Game "Official"?

Although each league has its own rules, in most situations a game has to go five innings before it can be an official game.

That's important in case it starts to rain during the course of your game. Once the game begins, only the umpires (not the coaches) can decide whether the game should be stopped.

Note: If the home team is winning, then the game only has to go four-and-a-half innings; after all, there's no need for the home team to bat in the bottom of the fifth if they're already winning.

"If they ever have Bowling Ball Night here, I'm definitely not coming."

JACK AKER
former Cleveland pitching coach after White Sox fans showered the Indians with seat cushions on "Seat Cushion Night" in Chicago

NOTES

_____

_____

_____

_____

_____

_____

_____

_____

SOURCES

BASEBALL...A LAUGHING MATTER, Warner Fusselle and
Rick Wolff, *The Sporting News*, St. Louis, 1987.